This book is dedicated to all who find Nature not an adversary to conquer and destroy, but a storehouse of infinite knowledge and experience linking man to all things past and present. They know conserving the natural environment is essential to our future well-being.

YELLOWSTONE
THE STORY BEHIND THE SCENERY®

Yellowstone National Park, located in the northwestern corner of Wyoming, was the first national park. Established in 1872, it preserves unparalled hydrothermal features.

by Hugh Crandall
Photography by David Muench

Hugh Crandall, since his retirement from the U.S. Navy, has contributed much toward helping Americans understand their national parks. At Yellowstone, Hugh served several years as interpretive consultant to the National Park Service and as director of the Yellowstone Institute. He has written two other books in this series: *Shenandoah* and *Grand Teton*.

David Muench's photography is featured in this book. One of our country's foremost landscape photographers, Dave's intimate knowledge of Yellowstone enabled him to capture the park at its finest.

Front cover: Old Faithful erupting at sunset. Photo by Ray Atkeson. Inside front cover: Minerva Terrace, Mammoth Hot Springs. Title page: Bighorn sheep. Pages 2/3: Grand Canyon of the Yellowstone. Photos by David Muench.

Book Design by K. C. DenDooven

Seventh Printing, 1990

Yellowstone — a strange, wonderful land where, as if in a fantasy, seething cauldrons and roaring infernos appear in scenes of cool, pastoral beauty. Here nature rules—untamed, uninhibited—yet serves man's need to know, in every sense, her magic and her power.

Yellowstone National Park is today just what it has always been—two million acres of virgin wilderness. The changes man has introduced affect only one percent of this vast area. Here, with only a little effort, it is possible to move away from buildings and blacktop to a place beyond the sensory impact of civilization. Alone for a moment or two in a world that has remained essentially unchanged for eight thousand years, one may come to feel a tingling kinship with one of those who were here at times long past—perhaps John Colter, as he explored these forests and mountains in 1807; or a stalking Shoshone of the years before Colter; or even one of the ancient hunters who, with his people, followed the game herds that moved into this high country as the ice receded.

Every visitor, no matter how casual, comes to know a little of Yellowstone's wildness. Inevitably he becomes aware of things not contemplated before—that a geyser erupts because it is a wild and natural thing that does what it must, and that the bear, moose, and elk are here because this is their natural habitat. He may reflect on how few are the people who have been to the bottom of Yellowstone Canyon or to the top of Mount Holmes. And he may come to appreciate, as he views the wild land and its wild inhabitants, how little of Yellowstone has *ever* felt the foot of man.

But the most significant aspect of Yellowstone National Park is probably not its wildness; it is something intangible and magical that lies in the name itself. The many unusual features of Yellowstone have been observed by millions of people; but, for every person who has watched Old Faithful erupt or has stood on the rim of the Grand Canyon of the Yellowstone River, there are dozens of others who have only seen photographs or heard the familiar names. All of these people have one thing in common; they share a special feeling—a pride of ownership—for Yellowstone, the world's first national park.

Had there been a human civilization anywhere to note the event, the volcanic eruption that formed the Yellowstone caldera may literally have been noticed throughout the earth—just as, since 1872, the thunder of the falls at Yellowstone, the hissing roar of Old Faithful, and the bugling of a bull elk have been figuratively "heard around the world," the sounds that have been recorded everywhere in acts of preservation and conservation.

This is the story of those sounds and of the wonders that cause them. And it is the story of another, perhaps even greater wonder: the national-park movement that they stimulated to conception.

Most of Yellowstone is a high plateau nearly encircled by mountain ranges of the northern Rockies. The average elevation of the relatively level central plateau is about 8,200 feet, and many of the surrounding peaks reach 10,000 to 11,000 feet. The park is situated just south of the forty-fifth parallel of latitude, halfway between the Equator and the North Pole. Because of its high elevation and northern latitude, its climate is characterized by

The Landscape

long, harsh winters and short, cool summers. Variations in elevation and differences in the arrangement of the mountains to the west of the park cause precipitation fluctuations from eight inches a year at the north entrance near Gardiner, Montana, to over seventy inches a year in the southwest corner. Many of the mountains and river valleys have the distinctive shapes of land that has been heavily glaciated.

Vegetation is primarily coniferous forest, but many of the wide valleys are covered predominantly by grasses, herbaceous plants, and small shrubs. The drier areas are typical northern desert characterized by sagebrush, junipers, and desert grasses. The tops of the higher mountains are thinly sheathed in alpine tundra above timberline. None of the mountains are snow-covered the year around, but most of them retain permanent

Hot-water runoff from the many geysers and hot springs along the Firehole keep the river ice-free in winter and make it a sanctuary for elk, bison, and waterfowl.

Hydrothermal features can be found almost anywhere in the park, but the greatest concentrations and varieties are located in the geyser basins at Norris and along the Firehole River.

patches of snow, like miniature glaciers, on the northern slopes. Interspersed here and there in the landscape are the many rivers and mountain brooks with their hundreds of breathtaking cascades and waterfalls, the dozens of clear, sparkling lakes, and the hydrothermal areas (geysers, hot springs, mud pots, and fumaroles) with their own peculiar terrain and vegetative characteristics.

This, then, is the landscape of Yellowstone National Park—a landscape that has been determined primarily by the rocks that underlie it and the forces that formed them.

UPON THESE ROCKS —

The age of the earth—according to the best information available to the scientific community —is about 4.7 billion years. But during the first 700 million of those years the earth was changing from an undifferentiated mass of interstellar debris to the layered arrangement of concentric spheres it is today, so the age of the earth in its present form is about four billion years. In Yellowstone National Park the oldest exposed rocks are 2.7 billion years old and the youngest rocks are being formed at this very moment. Thus the geologic story of Yellow-

stone spans nearly two-thirds of the life of the earth itself!

That's a very long story, even if told quickly! Most geologic action takes place very slowly, but in three billion years a great many events can happen. Much of what occurred in Yellowstone is the same, or nearly so, as that which has occurred elsewhere, but some of these developments, the subplots within the larger story, are unique to the Yellowstone scene.

For example, nowhere else in the world is there a larger or more varied collection of hydrothermal features. Yellowstone has more geysers, hot springs, mud pots, and fumaroles than all the rest of the world combined. The individual concentrations at Mammoth Hot Springs, Norris, and the geyser basins along the Firehole River are unsurpassed anywhere. *Why* are they here?

And about 600,000 years ago, over a thousand square miles of this part of the Rocky Mountains burst upward in one of the greatest explosions the earth has ever known. Again, we want to know *why.*

The answer to both "whys" is the same. It begins with a description of those concentric spheres into which the earth differentiated four billion years ago:

The outermost sphere is a thin layer of solidified rock which overlies the rest of the earth in much the way skin covers muscle and bone. This crust of rock averages about thirty miles thick where there are land masses and about ten miles thick under the oceans. Just beneath the crust is a very deep layer of the materials from which rocks are made. It is called the *mantle layer.* Thousands of miles thick, it reaches all the way to the innermost sphere, the core of the earth. The mantle layer is under great pressure from its own weight and the weight of the crust above it. Unlike the crust, it is not quite solid; nor is it entirely liquid. Its in-between state is best described as "plastic."

But a small portion of the mantle *is* liquid and, for reasons not yet fully understood, sometimes collects in pockets—like blisters under the skin of the crust. That liquid is molten rock, or *magma.* Above such concentrations the crust becomes thinner, partly because it has been stretched by the "blister" and partly because its lower edge has been melted by the molten rock beneath. Such a magma chamber underlies Yellowstone; the crust here, instead of being thirty or forty miles thick, is only three or four miles thick and is cracked from stretching!

It is that magma chamber, perhaps two hundred miles deep and lying only a few miles below the surface, that gradually built up the excessive pressure that resulted in the eruption of 600,000 years ago. Today the cracks resulting from that eruption allow surface water to seep down into the thin crust to the heated rock of its lower edge, become itself heated, and rise again to the surface, where it spurts out in geysers or flows out in hot springs. These two phenomena—the gigantic volcanic eruption and the extensive hydrothermal activity—are uniquely Yellowstone's. And each is a result of the presence beneath the park of that huge chamber of partially molten rock.

There is another geological feature of Yellowstone that is unmatched anywhere else—the fossil forests of Specimen Ridge. That, too, was the result of abrupt and violent volcanism, but of a much earlier time.

Volcanic-ash flows of rhyolitic material are sometimes welded together by pressure and their own heat into a rock called welded tuff. Pinnacled ridges such as this one are typical of the erosion pattern of mountains composed of tuff.

A glass-like rock called obsidian is formed when rhyolitic lava containing very little water cools quickly. Obsidian was used in Stone-Age America for tools and projectile points, and it was traded extensively. Artifacts of Yellowstone obsidian have been found as far east as Ohio.

THE VOLCANIC ERUPTION

When a magma chamber develops, the crustal rocks expand as they are heated to their melting point and beyond, so the magma is under pressure. As a result of that pressure the unmelted part of the crust may lift and crack above the chamber. Sometimes the magma will then force its way into the cracks, up to the surface, and flow out in streams and sheets now called *lava*. (Such flows have been known to cover huge areas, as those that formed the Columbia Plateau of Washington and Oregon and those that covered most of southern Idaho.) But at other times the pressure is released suddenly in an eruption that blasts molten rock high into the air. If the eruption is explosive enough, it will empty the magma from the upper part of the chamber, leaving the crust unsupported, except at the edges, like a "roof" over the magma remaining far below. If that roof caves in, it creates a special sort of volcanic crater, a *caldera*. This was the sequence of events that occurred here to create the Yellowstone caldera.

Over a large, elliptical area, lava and ash sprayed and flowed out of the vents and cracks in the stretched crust until the upper section of the magma chamber was emptied. The thin, rocky crust that remained could not support itself above the hollow space and—in one momentous cataclysm—a section of the earth's surface forty miles long and thirty miles wide collapsed and fell many thousands of feet into the pool of magma.

Such crustal collapses have occurred in many places throughout the world, but in few places has one been known to result in a caldera as extensive as Yellowstone's. It reaches from the Madison River to the eastern edge of Yellowstone Lake, and from Lewis Lake to the Upper Falls of the Yellowstone River. Whatever land forms may have existed before in the space to the west of the Absaroka Range and to the north of the Red Mountains were destroyed forever. The earth began to build anew.

During the millennia that followed, other eruptions occurred, and the lava flows issuing from them nearly filled the tremendous depression. Some lava even ran out of the caldera proper, escaping over low places in the wall. The Upper and Lower falls of the Yellowstone River drop from the edges of two such overflows. The Pitchstone Plateau in the southwest corner of the park is the remains of the latest flow, which took place only 60,000 years ago.

Because the caldera was so nearly buried, its existence was not even suspected until satellite photographs revealed its distinctive outline. Now

that we know it is there, the higher walls that were not covered by later outpourings become obvious at several places. The north wall of the Madison River canyon is part of the original wall of the caldera.

Those satellite photographs, together with other recent geological investigations, have disclosed an interesting aspect of the volcanic activity of this area. About two million years ago an eruption occurred that resulted in the collapse that formed the caldera extending from Island Park, Idaho, well into the central part of Yellowstone. Later, about 1.2 million years ago, a second caldera was formed near Island Park. And still later, about 600,000 years ago, the Yellowstone caldera was formed yet farther to the northeast. Recent geophysical measurements indicate that the underlying magma chamber may now be centered under the northeastern edge of the last caldera.

The theory of plate tectonics has been generally accepted as the explanation for the crustal activity of the earth. This is the belief that the huge crustal plates making up the earth's surface are slowly moving over the mantle layer beneath. The

Basaltic lava contracts as it cools, often cracking into four- to eight-sided shapes that become columns as the contracting and cracking continue. This particular example of "columnar jointing" is located near Tower Fall.

evidence of the three calderas and the present location of the magma chamber farther along an extension of the same line indicate the possibility that Yellowstone National Park is slowly but inexorably sliding toward the southwest.

The dates of the three eruptions (2 million, 1.2 million, and .6 million years ago, respectively) seem to suggest that sometime in the next one to two hundred thousand years the northeast corner of the park may become the fourth caldera. So, if you are planning to visit Cooke City or the Beartooth, be sure to do so within the next hundred thousand years!

THE STONE FOREST

After most of the Rocky Mountain cordillera had been formed during the thirty-million-year, mountain-building episode known as the Laramide orogeny, the land was still unstable enough to be subject to volcanic activity. So intermittent volcanism was the predominant character of another fifteen million years—volcanism that resulted in the Absaroka Range. During that time this area was lower than it is today—mountainous, yes, but mountains whose bases were closer to sea level. Also, the elevation, the rainfall, and the climate in general were right for the growth of deciduous trees, so that mixed hardwood forests and a few redwoods flourished here as the Absaroka volcanoes began to erupt.

Most of the eruptions were, volcanically speaking, mild flows of andesitic and basaltic lava. But some were explosive outpourings of volcanic ash and cinders. The materials of these flows engulfed the forest and, by shutting out the oxygen of the air, prevented the trees from burning. Mud flows also carried trees and stumps from higher elevations, mixing upland species with lowland species. During the millions of years since the trees were buried, the organic material of the original wood has been replaced, cell by cell, by the minerals of the rocks. Then the rock and soil that had covered the trees gradually eroded away to expose, still standing in their places, the petrified replicas of the sycamores, oaks, walnuts, magnolias, and dogwoods of that forest of forty-five million years ago.

These fossil forests, distributed over as much as 500 square miles, constitute one of the largest series of deposits of petrified plant remains in the world. Such an extensive deposit of an assemblage of climatic regimes bears further investigation. It also provides us with a window from which we can speculate into the past forty-five million years.

THE LAND SHAPERS: ICE

Powerful as the forces of volcanism and mountain building are, there is one natural force of the earth that is as great as both of them combined. That force is erosion, for four billion years keeping pace with the best that plate tectonics can do.

The strongest instrument of erosion is water, and it is still a powerful force in the form of ice. When winter snowfall year after year exceeds summer melt, the old snow becomes nearly as dense as solid ice, and when the buildup is hundreds or thousands of feet thick, the ice actually flows, both within itself and over the land. As it flows, stones the ice has plucked from the mountainsides are carried with it. Given time, a glacier can change the highest mountain to a scoured mound surrounded by beds of sand and gravel.

Yellowstone has been glaciated at least three times. All three known glacial periods coincide with extensive advances of the continental glaciers over North America. Although those giant sheets of ice did not extend as far south as the Wyoming Rockies, whatever the climatic change was that allowed them to spread all across Canada also allowed huge montane glaciers to develop in the mountains of this area.

The first of these three glacial periods began about 300,000 years ago and continued for over 100,000 years. The second began about 125,000 years ago and lasted for about 75,000 years. The

most recent glaciation reached its peak about 40,000 years ago and gradually receded. By 15,000 years ago (still 10,500 years before the first Egyptian pyramid was erected) the last glaciers had receded to a few small patches on the higher peaks, and pines, elk, and people were living in the Yellowstone area.

During the final, or Pinedale, glaciation the ice packs grew in the Absaroka Mountains to the north and to the southeast of the park. As these glaciers became larger and higher, the one to the north flowed south through Slough Creek and west through the Lamar and Yellowstone valleys. The one to the south flowed north through the upper Yellowstone valley, filled the Yellowstone Lake depression, and continued on down the Hay-den Valley. The two met and spread together almost to what is now the western boundary of the park. It is now known that the highest peaks (those as high or higher than Mount Washburn, for instance) were covered, and all the lowlands were frozen under thousands of feet of ice. The mountains were thinned and sharpened as the glaciers plucked stones from their sides, and the valleys were broadened and rounded as the ice gouged their floors and walls with those stones. Then, when the glaciers had dwindled away, the stones and silt were left as the new floors of the reshaped valleys. It is that sand and silt and gravel, spread evenly across a wide area, that causes Slough Creek and the upper Yellowstone to meander quietly through broad areas of sedges and willows.

Glaciers often plucked huge stones from the mountainsides and carried them many miles from the bedrock of which they were a part. Here they were abandoned as the last great glaciers melted away 15,000 years ago. These granite boulders, now half buried in the thin soil of the alpine tundra, are called "glacial erratics," because they are strangers to the area and are not related to the rocks beneath them.

Running water is the most erosive of all the forces of nature. The Yellowstone River is only one of the fast-flowing mountain streams that have made the Yellowstone country a network of stream-cut valleys. The same crystals that can now be seen shining on a mountainside may some day sparkle in beds of sand far out in the plains.

THE LAND SHAPERS: RUNNING WATER

Water in its usual state as a liquid is probably the factor most responsible for erosion. It dissolves some minerals and chemically alters others. It seeps into tiny cracks in rocks where, expanding as it freezes, it breaks boulders loose. But water is most erosive when it is moving, and the faster it moves the more it erodes. Even a slow, meandering stream carries tiny particles of silt and clay; a faster stream carries grains of sand; a rushing torrent moves rocks. The silt and sand and rocks abrade the stream bed to cut it deeper and in the process provide more material with which to cut more rock.

Yellowstone is typical of mountain areas with moderate to high rainfall. The abundance of precipitation is such that it cannot all be evaporated or utilized by the life forms of the area. The excess runs off and, because the mountains are steep, it runs off fast. So Yellowstone, except in the level central section where the rivers are slow, is a land of deeply cut stream valleys. The best known is the Grand Canyon of the Yellowstone River—its story is a saga in and of itself.

The Yellowstone River is in part at least two million years old. Until the eruption occurred that formed the Yellowstone caldera, it was much like several other rivers that were slowly cutting channels through the Absaroka volcanic rock. After the caldera was formed, the valley of the ancestral Yellowstone was choked with volcanic ash—a material that was hot enough when it settled to weld itself by its own heat and weight into a type of rock known as "welded tuff." The river became much smaller than it had been (and than it is now) because it now drained only the outer slope of the caldera rather than the large area it had drained before the volcanic eruption cut the river into two sections. The upper section of the river, with its headwaters high up on the slopes of Younts Peak to the southeast of the park, was dammed by the north rim of the caldera.

Nevertheless, the curtailed lower section of the river slowly began to recut its old channel

These pinnacles owe their shapes to two erosive forces: Water has widened the once-tiny cracks between them, and wind-blown sand has rounded the columns.

through the barricade of tuff. At the same time the upper section was draining into a depression among the lava flows that filled the caldera, thus forming a large lake. Finally the lake overflowed northward into the original lower section and the river was restored to its original length and size. The added water gave the river greater erosive power, and the down-cutting of its channel proceeded rapidly. It soon reached its former level in the canyon it had cut many years before through the Absaroka volcanics.

About 300,000 years ago, the development of the river was interrupted by 100,000 years of glaciation. Fortunately for our story and for the millions of people who have enjoyed the unique canyon that the river was yet to produce, the flow of the glacier was directed across the canyon rather than down it. Although the valley was filled with ice during each of the three glacial episodes, it was not materially shaped by glacial flow; it remained a V-shaped, stream-cut valley.

During the long ages of the first glaciation, another development occurred that was instrumental in making the canyon what it is today. All around the rim of the caldera are cracks in the crust, called *ring fractures*. For many thousands of years hot water and steam rose through those cracks and, for several miles below the present falls, the rhyolite was hydrothermally altered to a softer rock that eroded more easily and was yellow instead of the usual grey of unaltered rhyolite. So, during the 75,000 or so ice-free years before the next glaciation, the river cut quickly through the softer rock and by a little over 100,000 years ago, the Grand Canyon of the Yellowstone River was essentially completed (as much as any natural feature is ever completed). The river is still down-cutting its channel, and its falls are still being moved very slowly back toward the lake. But, unless there is another catastrophic event in this restless land, the canyon will appear much as it does today for another 100,000 years.

The Yellowstone River falls over a ledge of volcanic rock and cuts deeply into a section of the same rock— rock that has been chemically changed by steam and hot water.

Old Faithful erupts on a windless morning.

THE HYDROTHERMAL PHENOMENA

To have such activity as is implicit in the word *hydrothermal*, there must be water and heat. But also needed is a way to get the water to the heat and back again—a kind of "plumbing system." Yellowstone has the world's largest collection of hydrothermal features because it has the world's best combination of those three factors. It has an average of about forty inches of precipitation a year; there is a large body of magma close to the surface to heat the crustal rocks; the cracks in those rocks are deep enough to allow the rain and melting snow to reach the heat source; and the heat energy is great enough to force the water to return to ground level.

The temperature of the crust over most of the land areas of the world will increase about one degree Fahrenheit per hundred feet of depth. In the central section of Yellowstone, where most of the hydrothermal activity occurs, the United States Geological Survey has drilled several research wells from 500 feet to 1,100 feet deep. Thermometers lowered into the wells indicate that the average temperature at 500 to 600 feet deep is above 400 degrees Fahrenheit!

At the 7,500-foot average elevation of the Yellowstone plateau, water boils at 199 degrees, instead of the 212 degrees needed at sea level. But deep in the ground the water is under such pressure from the rocks and water above it that it can become much hotter than the normal boiling point without changing from liquid to gas. (The water in a teakettle gets no hotter than the boiling point at its elevation, but the water in a pressure cooker can be considerably hotter.) It is believed the water in some areas of the park percolates quickly enough through porous rock layers to allow it to reach depths of 10,000 feet or more before becoming hot enough for convection to cause the water to start its return journey. At such depths the pressure is very great and the water can become very hot, so that when it starts to rise and the pressure is reduced, some of it flashes into steam, increasing its volume and causing it to rise faster than convection alone would have carried it. At about that point a process has begun that nothing, other than mixing with cooler surface waters, can stop; it can end only when the water is released at or near the surface.

The routes by which the water reaches its equilibrium at the surface and the form in which it emerges are entirely a matter of plumbing. If there is a large, smooth route available, it will spill out as a "constant gusher." If there is a pool into which it rises, it usually will result on the surface as a *hot spring*. But if there are cavities and restrictions in

Silica that has been dissolved in hot water precipitates as the water cools here in Grotto Geyser in the Upper Geyser Basin. The silica is deposited on the surface in the form of sinter, or geyserite. Building at a rate of approximately one inch per hundred years, it creates fanciful mounds around the geyser outlet.

the plumbing system, it possibly will become a *geyser*, and the flow will be intermittent because after each eruption the cavities in the system must fill up before another eruption can take place. But, regardless of plumbing, the water will eventually reach the surface again, even if it is only as steam rising from a fumarole or bubbling through a mud pot. When it does, its temperature will usually be back to 199 degrees or lower, the water having traded its heat energy for the kinetic energy required to lift it back to ground level.

The eruption patterns of hydrothermal features may change from year to year. The changes may result from variations in the availability of surface water. More often they are the result of alterations in the underground ducts through which the cold water reaches the heated rock or through which the hot water returns to the surface. Such modifications sometimes are caused by earthquakes, which are common in areas such as Yellowstone where recent volcanism has occurred.

The most frequent cause of hydrothermal changes, though, lies in the nature of water itself. Water is the most versatile of all the common chemicals of our world. It is one of the few compounds that can exist as a gas, a liquid, or a solid within a temperature range tolerable to living things. Most elements and compounds are, to some extent at least, soluble in water—particularly hot water. So, as superheated water passes through the substrata, at least a small amount of the rock is dissolved, and the shapes and sizes of the conduits are gradually

Emerald Pool in the Upper Geyser Basin reflects the encircling lodgepole pines.

The red streaks are algae and bacteria, growing in the runoff channels of this hot spring on the shore of Yellowstone Lake at West Thumb.

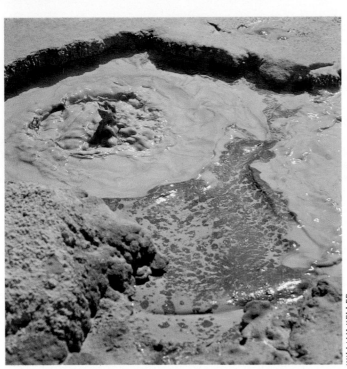

Mud pots are hot springs that produce a quantity of water that is too small to flush away the material they bring to the surface.

altered. If the hot water dissolves enough of the minerals to become saturated with them, as it cools on its way to the surface it will be supersaturated and some of the dissolved minerals will be deposited on the walls of the upper channels, thus altering that part of the plumbing system too. The wonder of Old Faithful is not so much that it works, but that it has continued to work in much the same way and at much the same rhythm for more than a hundred years.

The reliability of Old Faithful's eruptive pattern can be attributed to a large extent to the com-position of the rock through which its water passes. It is hard rock, composed generally of minerals that are almost insoluble, even in hot water. So deposits build up very slowly and the changes to the duct system are slight. Nevertheless, as the waters of the geysers along the Firehole River percolate through the silica-rich rhyolite that underlies the area, some of the silica is dissolved and redeposited as the water cools. The new form of silica, called *sinter* or *geyserite*, is laid down at the rate of about an inch every hundred years, and persistent geysers are thus gradually building their

Part of the plumbing system of Morning Glory Pool in Upper Geyser Basin is easily visible through the clear water.

because the water in the system does not have quite enough energy to lift itself all the way up. Hillside openings are frequently only fumaroles. Sometimes the pool from which the steam is rising can be heard boiling far underground.

Although there are only the four basic types of hydrothermal features (geysers, hot springs, mud pots, and fumaroles) there is an infinite variety within each category. Shapes, sizes, flow rates, colors, temperatures—all vary. And all these examples tell us more about the fascinating geological phenomena by which tomorrow's rocks are being built right before our eyes.

distinctive cones. The small geyserite pebbles that can be found near the cones are known as "geyser eggs." They are probably formed by surface agitation of particles at or in shallow pools near the vent.

In the Mammoth Hot Springs area the buildup of hydrothermal deposits is many times faster because the mineral is different. Thick beds of limestone, a mineral that is highly soluble in water, underlie Mammoth. The dissolved calcium carbonate of the limestone and other sedimentary rocks is redeposited as *travertine* at such a rapid rate that careful observation can detect changes from week to week. The underground ducts and passages are modified so quickly that the most active spring this year may next year be only a trickle emerging from a collapsed heap of travertine rubble. Year after year deeply buried beds of limestone are being transported to the surface. The travertine at Mammoth is now many feet thick and makes up a large part of Terrace Mountain.

A special kind of hot spring results when the available water is limited and acidic. What water there is dissolves and chemically alters the minerals of the underground rocks, carrying the products to the surface as small particles. But there is not enough water to wash the particles away. Held in suspension by the small amount of water and steam that continue to bubble up, they collect in pools of mud and clay—*mud pots* and *mud volcanoes.*

Fumaroles—openings from which only steam and other gases emerge—are the fourth general category of hydrothermal features. They develop

ANATOMY OF A LIMESTONE HOT SPRING

At Mammoth Hot Springs rain or melted snow sinks deep into the earth, perhaps as much as two miles, through porous rock layers and cracks in the earth's crust. At that depth the water, under great pressure from its own weight, encounters rock that has been heated by the underlying partially molten rock that lies a few miles below much of Yellowstone's surface. The water is heated far above the normal surface boiling point, and convection currents force it back to the surface through other cracks. It also absorbs volcanic gases, principally carbon dioxide, and becomes "carbonated" water, a weak carbonic-acid solution. The rising water passes through layers of limestone, dissolving some in the hot carbonic acid. But the water cools on its way up and can no longer hold as much material in solution. At the surface, then, the carbon dioxide is released into the air, and the dissolved limestone is precipitated as the "travertine" that makes up Terrace Mountain and the fanciful formations of the hot-spring terraces. Over two tons of travertine are deposited here by rising waters each day.

Minerva Terrace at Mammoth Hot Springs is an outstanding example of the many patterns that travertine forms as it is deposited on the surface by the cooling water of a hot spring. Minerva has been called "a limestone cave turned inside out."

THE GEOLOGIC CHRONOLOGY

What happened in Yellowstone before about half a billion years ago is not actually known; the evidence that might have told the story has been thoroughly obscured by subsequent events. But there are rocks in Yellowstone that have been dated as over 2.5 billion years old. Some of them were once granite, an igneous rock formed deep in the crust, and some were once sandstone, a sedimentary rock formed from deposits laid down under bodies of water. So it can be fairly assumed that for most of its 4.6 billion years the earth has been going on its way, doing much the same things it does today. It has made mountains and worn them down again. It has raised continents out of the oceans and lowered them again beneath the water. It has known long periods during which large areas have been covered by thousands of feet of ice. It has had times of intense volcanic activity. And it has known millions of years of peace. So much for the first four billion years.

About 570 million years ago most of what is now western United States, including the land where Yellowstone now lies, was covered by shallow seas. From then until seventy-five million years ago nothing much happened except that the sea repeatedly receded and returned—all in all a pretty quiet half a billion years.

Then a restless period began that has lasted all the way to the present. First there were thirty million years of landfolding and mountain building that resulted in the three-thousand-mile chain that is the Rocky Mountains. Then there were the nearly fifteen million years of volcanic activity that produced Bunsen Peak, Mount Washburn, and the rest of the Absaroka Range. This period seems to have been followed by a recess in the restlessness —a lull that lasted for twenty-five million years.

Ten million years ago that interlude of relative inactivity ended when the whole region began to be uplifted far above its former level. The crust was cracked into blocks that shifted against one another, some continuing upward and some subsiding. The Gallatin Range was formed from an uplifted block a hundred miles long and twenty miles wide. Chicken Ridge in the south of the park was displaced 15,000 feet. South of Yellowstone the Teton Range and Jackson Hole shifted against one another a distance of more than 30,000 feet.

That is not to say the Tetons were ever 30,000 feet above the surrounding land. When mountains are uplifted, erosion becomes very rapid and usually keeps pace with the uplift. The fault-block mountains may never have been any higher than

Hydrothermal features seem almost infinitely varied. The obsidian sand at Black Sand Geyser Basin is one of the most remarkable of these variations.

Tower Creek is cutting its channel more slowly than the Yellowstone River is down-cutting its own. The creek joins the Yellowstone by dropping from a ledge of hard rock as the beautiful Tower Fall.

they are today.

The last two million years have seen renewed volcanic activity that began with the Huckleberry Ridge caldera formation and ended perhaps with the Pitchstone Plateau flow of 70,000 years ago. During that time the area also has experienced three periods of intensive glaciation. For the last ten or twelve thousand years, the principal geological activity has been the final melting of the glaciers, many noticeable earthquakes, the continuing hydrothermal performances, and the ever-present erosion as the earth follows its continuing cycle of erasing its creations and building new ones.

Algae vividly color hot-spring runoff areas.

Overleaf: Minerva Terrace, Mammoth Hot Springs

SUGGESTED READING

FRITZ, WILLIAM J. Roadside Geology of the Yellowstone Country. Missoula, Montana: Mountain Press Publishing Co., 1985.

KEEFER, WILLIAM R. The Geologic Story of Yellowstone National Park. Yellowstone National Park: Yellowstone Library and Museum Association, 1976.

MARLER, G. D. The Story of Old Faithful. Yellowstone National Park: Yellowstone Library and Museum Association, 1969.

PARSONS, WILLARD H. Middle Rockies and Yellowstone. Dubuque, Iowa: Kendall/Hunt Publishing Co., 1978.

Life at Yellowstone

The history of the present life communities of Yellowstone is relatively short. It begins with the end of the last glacial period, between eight and twelve thousand years ago. That four-thousand-year interval is not a span used as an approximation, it is the amount of time it actually took for the last ice age in this area to come to an end. Glaciation neither begins nor ends suddenly; it takes many years (in this case, thousands) for massive ice packs to either form or melt away.

Temperature is a factor in determining both the onset of glaciation and the rate at which a region recovers when glaciation is over. But the climatic changes that result in such vast accumulations of ice do not necessarily have to be large. The year-round average temperature of most of Yellowstone is thirty-five degrees. If that average were to drop only three degrees, another glacial buildup could begin. Or, if the annual snowfall were to increase by a foot or two, ice packs could develop even without a change in temperature. But in either case the new conditions would have to persist for thousands of years in order to produce another glacial epoch. And, if those slight changes were then reversed and present conditions restored, it again would take thousands of years for the masses of ice to recede to the highest peaks and disappear.

Because the changes in climate were slight during the long periods that ice covered this high country, conditions at the surrounding lower elevations were not much different from those that exist today. There were trees and grasses and flowers; there were mice and deer and elk and coyotes. The aspens turned golden in the fall, and moose grazed the underwater plants of the marshy meadows in the spring. When the ice-covered land in the high country was again ready for life, the seeds of that life were available from these nearby sources. For four thousand years, as the tongues of ice receded, they were closely followed by an advancing wave of green.

One of the carriers of plant seeds is the wind, and the prevailing wind in this area is from the southwest, so most of Yellowstone's present plant life probably migrated onto these high plateaus from the Snake River plains. Likewise, that region is believed to have been seeded at some earlier time by the wind which blew through the funnel of the Columbia River Valley from the Cascade Mountains of the Pacific Northwest. There is a resemblance between Yellowstone's vegetative cover and that of central Washington and Oregon, perhaps the result of that migratory route—the Oregon Trail in reverse.

But plants can spread, even against a prevailing wind, much faster than glaciers can recede—provided there is a suitable habitat into which their populations can expand. Perhaps the nature of Yellowstone's plant community is less the result of the prevailing winds than of the compatibility of the conditions here with the life-support requirements of the species, for some of the Pacific Northwest species are conspicuously absent. For example, the most widespread pine of the western United States is the ponderosa pine, and many exist in the Cascades; yet there are none in Yellowstone and none in the Snake River drainage area. If wind-driven propagation had been the sole basis for distribution, the ponderosa pine would now be common in southern Idaho and northwestern Wyoming. But it is not. Some other factor, then, must be limiting its spread into these areas. That limiting factor is not known at this time, although the characteristically low rainfall in May from year to year has been suggested as an explanation. Whatever the reason, the absence of the ponderosa cannot be explained by migration patterns. It just does not seem to like it here.

So, generally, it may be best to say that the twelve hundred or more kinds of higher plants that inhabit Yellowstone are here because they *do* like it —because conditions here are right for their growth and reproduction, and they can perpetuate their populations.

And there is one species that must *really* like it here. There are only eleven kinds of trees in the park, even though eighty percent of its area is

forested. And eighty percent of the forested area is made up of a single species, the lodgepole pine! To know the lodgepole pine, then, is to know two-thirds of the vegetative cover of Yellowstone National Park. (And to know the vegetation of an area is a good start to knowing the entire life community, for it is those green plants which provide the basis of that community.)

THE LODGEPOLE FOREST COMMUNITY

Most of Yellowstone is between 7,600 feet and 8,400 feet in elevation, has an annual precipitation of twenty to forty inches, and has soils derived from rhyolitic bedrock. That is the realm of the lodgepole pine. Its scientific name is *Pinus contorta* because on the Pacific coast, where it was first identified, it is a short, stout, twisted tree with a ragged crown. Here it grows slim and tall and straight—well-suited as a support (the lodgepole) for the hide-roofed lodges and tepees in which the native Indian once lived. So, depending on your location, you will find either the scientific name or the common name appropriate, but not both.

Two varieties of lodgepole pine exist in Yellowstone. The cones remain on both varieties for a period of three or four years. On one of these the cones open the second year, like most pines, and the seeds are released for dispersal. But the cones of the other variety are sealed by secretions of pitch and remain closed until heated enough for the pitch to melt. When fires sweep through a stand of closed-cone lodgepoles, the trapped seeds are released and regeneration can occur. Thus fire becomes an important factor in their survival.

In the spruce-fir forests of higher elevations the lodgepole pine is but a stage in the vegetational succession that ultimately gives way to the final stage—spruces and firs. But at the middle elevations where the pine is dominant there are large stands of the open-cone variety that seem to represent a climax vegetative type. These pines do not "nurse" some other species that is destined to replace them; instead they regenerate themselves and remain a forest that is predominantly lodgepole pine.

Any forest dominated by a single plant species is the home of only a few species of animals. But among the few living in the lodgepole forest community one can find red squirrels, snowshoe hares, porcupines, red-backed voles, nuthatches, pine siskins, hairy woodpeckers, Clarks nutcrackers, and two beautiful members of the weasel family—the pine marten and the ermine. Coyotes, lynxes, bobcats, bears—and an occasional wolverine—range through the lodgepole forest.

A forest of lodgepole pine covers nearly two-thirds of Yellowstone. It can vary from a dense stand of tall, thin trees—so close together that a dead tree has no place to fall—to an open, park-like woods carpeted by grass and wildflowers.

In the higher, colder areas of Yellowstone, spruce-fir forests predominate. The snow-covered tree in the foreground is a spruce, indicated by its pendant cones. Fir cones stand upright, like candles on a Christmas tree.

THE SPRUCE-FIR FOREST COMMUNITY

At elevations above 8,400 feet it is colder than at lower levels; the precipitation is usually above forty inches; and the bedrock is usually basaltic or andesitic—rocks richer than rhyolite in minerals. For one or more of these reasons the lodgepole pine gives way to the subalpine fir and Englemann spruce. But not entirely. Pines are "pioneer" trees of the spruce-fir forest, an earlier stage in the vegetative succession. So there are few stands of only spruce or only fir or even of mixed spruce and fir. At lower elevations of their range they usually are mixed with lodgepole pine, and at the upper limits they share the forest with whitebark pine, a common timberline tree of this part of the Rocky Mountains.

Most of the birds and mammals of the lodge-pole pine forest can be found in the spruce-fir forest as well. But in the more varied forests of the higher elevations the western jumping mice and northern flying squirrels also live.

THE ALPINE TUNDRA COMMUNITY

As elevation increases, temperature decreases, at the rate of about five degrees Fahrenheit per thousand feet. So, as far as life communities are concerned, to climb a thousand feet is about equal to going northward three hundred miles. Eventually, by either climbing higher or by traveling farther northward, you can reach climatic conditions that will not support trees. In the north the vast treeless plains are known by the Russian word *tundra*. In Yellowstone the same arctic conditions prevail at elevations above about 10,000 feet and the vegetative cover of sedges, grasses, and alpine flowers is called *alpine tundra*.

Because the terrain is usually steeper and the soil layer thinner at the higher elevations, there are many almost barren places of stony outcrops and rock slides. These seemingly inhospitable habitats are the homes of the pika, the yellow-bellied marmot, and the golden-mantled ground squirrel. The high, treeless islands of the alpine tundra community are the summer homes of the bighorn sheep and the feeding areas of the mountain bluebird. Mount Washburn is probably the easiest-to-reach example of this habitat. The summer herd of forty to fifty bighorn usually will contain a dozen or so lambs. Bluebirds hover motionless on the mountain updrafts and the panoramic views are magnificent.

THE MARSHLAND COMMUNITY

Many of the stream valleys of Yellowstone have been leveled and broadened by glaciers and subsequently floored by glacial sediment. As a result, their streams meander slowly and the land is marshy most of the year. Although their vegetation of tufted hair-grass, sedges, and willow shrubs is not particularly striking, these open valleys provide some of the most pleasant vistas in the park. They also provide habitats for some of the more interesting wildlife. Perhaps they can even take much of the credit for the existence of an established park here. If those marshy valleys had not supported the beavers that enticed trappers here, there may have been fewer of the oft-repeated tales of wonders that inspired the explorers who first promoted the park idea.

The beaver population has declined, but the valleys remain to provide homes for otters and muskrats and water birds. They are the breeding grounds of frogs, the feeding grounds of moose, and the fishing holes of bears.

THE SAGEBRUSH-GRASSLAND COMMUNITY

The lower elevations of the northern section of the park are in the rain shadow of the Gallatin Range to the west and thus receive less than twenty inches of rainfall a year. The slopes above the river bottoms are sheathed in sagebrush and various grasses suited to dry, porous soils. This is the summer range of the pronghorn and the winter range of a large number of bison and most of the

Bighorn sheep are one of the six species of large herbivores in Yellowstone. Older rams like these congregate, during most of the year, in small groups apart from the ewes and yearlings.

The Yellowstone high country is a land of flower-filled meadows nestled among jagged mountain peaks.

northern elk herd. This, too, is a place in which to find marmots, jackrabbits, and Uinta ground squirrels. It is the best area in which to see hawks and golden eagles and the most likely area in which to see a coyote or a badger.

THE NORTHERN DESERT COMMUNITY

A small section of Yellowstone near Mammoth Hot Springs and the town of Gardiner, Montana, receives even less than twenty inches of precipitation a year. Gardiner averages about eight inches and Mammoth, a thousand feet higher and five miles farther southeast, gets about fourteen inches. As a result of the low rainfall, the region is typical of northern desert areas. The grass is sparse and interspersed with big sagebrush and prickly pear. The occasional tree is usually a Rocky Mountain juniper.

Bighorn sheep winter on the crags and benches above the Gardiner and the Yellowstone rivers. During the October rutting season of the rams, the slopes of Mount Everts echo the loud, hollow clacks of their colliding horns. Pronghorn, mule deer, and elk are also common winter residents, probably attracted by the milder temperatures and the relatively light snow cover.

The watery world of the moose

The rocky haven of a marmot

THE AQUATIC COMMUNITIES

About ten percent of Yellowstone's surface is water. Yellowstone Lake is only one, albeit the largest, of hundreds of lakes and ponds, and the Yellowstone River is similarly only one of hundreds of rivers and streams. Each lake and river, even each section of the many bodies and strips of water, has its own unique life community. There are small, shallow ponds choked with cattails, rushes, and algae. There are swift torrents of clear, cold water. But none are without life. Even the smallest and the fastest will have its population of fish, the insect larvae on which fish feed, and the algae and bacteria which support the insects.

Together, the fish-bearing waters of Yellowstone make up one of the world's great fresh-water fisheries. The National Park Service and the U.S. Fish and Wildlife Service cooperate in its management to ensure its continuance as a natural element here. Fishing by people is carefully regulated in order to allow fishing by otters and eagles and ospreys and bears to go on as it always has, but even though the park visitor's catch is limited, he may still add a meal of freshly caught trout to his outdoor experience.

A special element of the aquatic environment of Yellowstone is the white pelican rookery on the Molly Islands—two small islands deep in the southeast arm of Yellowstone Lake. There are only seven white pelican breeding areas in North America, and these islands constitute the only one that lies within a national park.

Human activity seems to disrupt the breeding of white pelicans; thus the expansion of the human population may be the primary cause of a serious decrease in pelican numbers. So the historical nesting area of this great white bird is protected with special care. Landing on the rookery islands is prohibited, and motor boats are not allowed in the southernmost three miles of the lake.

Two of Yellowstone's distinctive habitats are the hot-spring home of the algae and the Yellowstone Lake home of the cutthroat trout. A third life community—the pine forests—covers the distant mountainsides.

White swans accent a snow-rimmed pond. The ice-free waters of Yellowstone support permanent populations of swans, ducks, and Canada geese.

THE HYDROTHERMAL COMMUNITIES

Some of the most unusual features of the already unusual hydrothermal areas of Yellowstone are the ecosystems for which their hot water and minerals provide the basis. Water at sea level boils at 212 degrees; the temperature of the coffee we cautiously sip is about 140 degrees; our bath water is usually less than 110 degrees. But there are bacteria that can thrive in water that is hotter than boiling! And some blue-green algae are able to live in water at a temperature of 165 degrees! The spectrum of colors that is frequently seen in the hydrothermal waters of Yellowstone is only rarely the result of mineral deposits such as iron oxides or sulfur compounds. Those rainbow colors are usually caused by living organisms!

In the thermal waters, as is true nearly anywhere, life attracts life. The blue-green algae (which, incidentally, can be many colors besides blue or green) and the true algae of the slightly cooler waters produce chlorophyll that uses the radiant energy of light to transform inorganic materials into the chemical energy of food compounds. Where there is food there is usually something to eat it. So a host of small, unusually heat-tolerant flies feed on the algae. They, in turn, are food for other flies, spiders, beetles, wasps, and the kildeer. As the plant-eating flies and their fly-eating predators die, their remains often fall in the water and are decomposed by bacteria. Thus the food chain of the thermal ecosystem completes a cycle and begins again.

During winter the thermal areas become islands of warmth in a sea of harsh cold. Beside the run-off channels the yellow monkey flower can sometimes be seen blooming in the snow. The bison and elk of the Firehole River drainage move into the geyser basins during extreme cold or after heavy snows. Elk and mule deer forage near the run-offs of the hot springs at Mammoth. Ponds and streams kept ice-free by the input of warm water become winter feeding areas for ducks, geese, and swans.

THE LARGE HERBIVORES

Many animals range daily, or in yearly migratory travels, through several life communities. The scavenger birds, the predatory birds, and the large predatory mammals rarely confine their activities to an area dominated by a single vegetative type. They get their food where they can find it and they range widely in the search. The same is true of the large herbivores.

Only thirteen species of wild ungulates are native to North America; six of these are represented in Yellowstone by free-ranging populations. The mule deer, the bighorn sheep, the pronghorn, the moose, the bison, and the American elk are neither fed nor fenced nor herded nor hunted in the park. They have complete freedom—including the freedom to leave or to be killed by a grizzly or

The American elk is the most numerous of the large herbivores in Yellowstone. These cow elk, bedded down for the night in a quiet pasture beside Obsidian Creek, may be part of the "northern herd," which numbers at least 16,000 animals.

a cougar. Severe winters are the major factor that controls their populations. Grizzly bears are taking full advantage of the large number of elk in the park, killing calves in spring and bulls in the fall. Bison are now hunted when they leave the park and move into Montana.

There is an almost magical efficiency about what Thoreau called "wildness." The natural world is not humane; indeed, it appears to be callously indifferent to the welfare of individuals. But it seems to work well toward the preservation of species. When food is abundant in a suitable habitat, populations increase. When food becomes scarce, the birth rate drops, predator populations increase (because *their* food supply becomes weaker and therefore more plentiful), and the undernourished animals become subject to disease and severe weather. The population drops to a level that matches the available food. Because population dynamics does not include instant reaction time, numbers usually will fall and rise in a cyclic swing. But, controlled by the "magic of wildness," the average will represent a stable compatibility within the ecosystem between the producers and the consumers. Only the introduction of a new factor, a change in the physical environment or the addition of a new organism, may result in a profound rearrangement of interrelationships within the community.

Archeological evidence indicates that the elk has inhabited North America for over 100,000 years and that it has been in the Yellowstone area for at least 12,000 years. But for a while during the last hundred years people believed that the Yellowstone elk could not survive on its own. So they tried various game-management practices—such as winter feeding, the elimination of predators, and systematic population reduction. It is now felt that the animals of a large national park, since they are not a resource to be harvested, may not need man's help except to protect them from man himself. So, given protection from hunters and the destruction of its habitat, the elk may still be able to manage on its own, just as it has done for a hundred thousand years.

The twenty-five to thirty thousand elk that summer in the park separate in winter into several herds. Of the major herds, only the Madison-Gibbon-Firehole elk remain entirely within park boundaries all year. Parts of the Gallatin and northern herds migrate out onto private or Forest Service lands in winter, where they are hunted. The entire southern herd migrates into Jackson Hole for the winter, and is hunted during its fall migration. On the elk preserve near Jackson this herd is fenced away from adjoining farm lands and pro-

Since the park's garbage dumps have been closed and roadside feeding discouraged, the bears of Yellowstone have been living as nature intended, deep in the wilderness areas.

Yellowstone supports one of the few surviving populations of the majestic bison. This small herd lives the year around in the grasslands of Hayden Valley.

This group of relaxed black bears may be a family—a mother and her yearling cubs.

vided supplemental food.

The winter ranges of the mule deer and pronghorn also extend slightly onto nonpark lands; numbers vary according to winter severity. Traditional bighorn winter ranges are inside or adjacent to the park. Moose are not herd animals, but most of the Yellowstone moose live out their lives within the park because they can cope with much deeper snow than other ungulates.

For over a hundred years the large mammals of Yellowstone have been one of its principal attractions, and for nearly a hundred years the preservation of that resource has been a management problem for the park. With a lot of help from the tendency of natural systems to restore themselves, and despite several well-intentioned measures that proved to be mistakes, that effort continues to be successful. The world of Yellowstone has been enjoyed by six generations of people and still remains essentially a place unspoiled, where future generations can experience that same wondrous world.

Black bears and grizzly bears were components of the Yellowstone ecosystem long before there was a park here. Because of the intense fascination people have always had for these large, fearless animals, the bears were exploited as tourist attractions for a very long period of time—from the 1870s well into the 1960s. They were baited to come into flood-lighted garbage dumps and special feeding stations (until the 1940s) to provide after-dinner entertainment for park visitors. And, despite a regulation against it, visitors were allowed to feed the bears that waited along the roads for hand-outs. The result was that Yellowstone bears, wilderness animals by nature, could not resist the temptation to move closer to the small enclaves of civilization and depend upon humans for part of their food.

Eventually it was realized that the proximity of the bears to humans was not a good thing. It was dangerous to humans and it was disruptive to the bears' natural way of life. A panhandling, junk-fed bear is not compatible with the wilderness concept.

So, in the early 1970s, the garbage dumps were closed and the regulation against feeding began to be enforced. Some bears, grown accustomed to living on human refuse, continued to harass people; these bears had to be trapped and moved, when possible, or eliminated altogether if gentler procedures failed. Now the bears have resumed their natural lives as wild creatures of a wild world.

Viable, self-sustaining populations of both the grizzly and the black bear still inhabit Yellowstone.

Few racks of antlers are as impressive as those of a bull wapiti.

Unless you are a back-country hiker, however, you are less likely to see a bear today than you were a few years ago. But the one you do see will be truly wild. Its life habits will be little changed from those of its ancestor, who shared his world with mammoths and sabre-toothed tigers.

SUGGESTED READING

Brock, Thomas D., and M. Louise. *Life in the Geyser Basins.* Yellowstone, Wyoming: Yellowstone Library and Museum Association, 1971.

Craighead, Karen. *Large Mammals of Yellowstone and Grand Teton National Parks.* Yellowstone, Wyoming: Yellowstone Library and Museum Association, 1978.

Despain, Don, and others. *Wildlife in Transition: Man and Nature on Yellowstone's Northern Range.* Boulder, Colorado: Roberts, Rinehart, Inc., 1986.

Follett, Richard F. *Birds of Yellowstone and Grand Teton National Parks.* Yellowstone, Wyoming: Yellowstone Library and Museum Association, 1976.

Meagher, Margaret Mary. *The Bison of Yellowstone National Park.* Washington, D.C.: U.S. National Park Service, 1973.

Schullery, Paul. *The Bears of Yellowstone.* Rev. and enl. ed. Boulder, Colorado: Roberts, Rinehart, Inc., 1986.

Shaw, Richard J. *Plants of Yellowstone and Grand Teton National Parks.* Salt Lake City: Wheelwright Press, Ltd., 1974.

Varley, John, and Paul Schullery. *Freshwater Wilderness: Yellowstone Fishes and Their World.* Yellowstone, Wyoming: Yellowstone Library and Museum Association, 1983.

Man at Yellowstone

The human history of Yellowstone National Park differs from the histories of most other national parks. In those other areas life preceded humanity by thousands or millions of years; in Yellowstone the history of man begins at very nearly the same time as the histories of other life forms. Until about 12,000 years ago the region lay under glacial ice, essentially with no life. Then, when the great mountain glaciers melted away in the warmer climate, living things from the surrounding lands began to homestead the glacial soil thus exposed. First the green plants moved in, then the plant-eaters, and then the meat-eating predators—including man.

The earliest evidence of man to have been found so far in the upper Yellowstone Valley has been dated at about 9,500 years ago, but the nature of that evidence indicates that people had probably been using this part of the world for many years before that. Those early people were nomadic hunters and gatherers who moved with the herds of herbivores that in turn moved with the seasons—just as today's herds do. Perhaps at a time about 10,000 years before these people drifted into this world, their ancestors crossed the Arctic land bridge from Asia. In their efforts to survive as one frail component of the vast North American ecosystem, they had moved ever southward along the coast and eastward in the paths of the receding glaciers.

Apparently those who reached this region— and their descendants for many centuries—made little use of this high country except during the mild seasons. Even modern man with all his technological advantages finds the Yellowstone plateau an inhospitable place in winter. The only people who seem to have made this world their home year around were a small group of Shoshone. Their culture was not affected by the introduction of the horse into the West in the seventeenth century, because they never acquired horses. Perhaps they had no opportunity to acquire them; perhaps they realized horses wouldn't be of much help in a place that lay deep in snow for half the year; or perhaps they were just conservative. Whatever the reason, the Shoshone remained foot travelers; and, although their numbers dwindled, they stayed in their simple encampments here until 1871, when they joined their kinsmen on the Shoshone Wind River Reservation.

Apparently the bighorn sheep was an important part of the Shoshone diet, a fact included in the reports of early trappers and explorers and borne out by the archaeological evidence of the kitchen middens at Indian hearth sites. Perhaps, for men on foot, armed only with primitive stone weapons, it was the easiest large game to kill. In any event, they were known generally as "Sheepeaters." They and their culture are now gone.

Another way in which Yellowstone's history differs from those of other national parks is simply because Yellowstone was the first. The history of any other park begins at the point in time when people began to think of that area as a possible national park. The history of Yellowstone, though, must include the development of the park concept itself, a history that in turn must include the entire record of man's changing attitudes toward the natural world. According to Aubrey Haines, the leading Yellowstone historian, that is a span of time that must extend as far back, at least, as Nebuchadezzar's Hanging Gardens of Babylon!

But the vast web of cause and effect that constitutes the workshop and the playground of the professional historian is far beyond the scope of this account. Instead we will begin with the first explorers in the early nineteenth century and will follow the events and attitudes that since then have contributed directly to the nature of Yellowstone as it is today. Those events group themselves into four distinct periods, each one characterized by the influence of particular segments of American society.

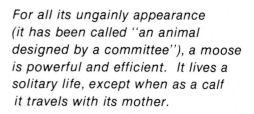
For all its ungainly appearance (it has been called "an animal designed by a committee"), a moose is powerful and efficient. It lives a solitary life, except when as a calf it travels with its mother.

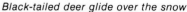
Black-tailed deer glide over the snow.

A beaver emerges from the water.

1805 TO 1865: THE SCOUTS AND TRAPPERS

The exploring party led by Lewis and Clark bypassed the Yellowstone country to the north but heard of some of its features from Indians they met along the way. John Colter, a member of that expedition, obtained permission to leave the party on its return and, in the interest of establishing trade relations with new groups of Indians, set out to explore the land south of the earlier route. In the autumn of 1807 or the spring of 1808, he was the first recorded white American to travel Yellowstone and to see the wonders of the area. Between those years and 1840, when the fur trade collapsed because the beaver hat went out of style, a considerable number of trappers came to know the Yellowstone country and its Indians, both friendly and hostile. From the demise of the fur trade to the close of the Civil War, there was only occasional penetration of this area, and most of that was done by prospectors in futile searches for gold.

1866 TO 1885: THE IDEALISTS AND THE OPPORTUNISTS

The scattered tales and reports of the unusual nature of the country at the headwaters of the Yellowstone and Snake rivers had fascinated the romantics among two generations of people. Finally, as gold fever abated and the Civil War ended, some of them found time to investigate for themselves. Between 1869 and 1872 two private expeditions and two others funded by Congress explored that allegedly wondrous land and reported in detail.

These reports confirmed earlier claims that the hydrothermal features and the Yellowstone Canyon were indeed wondrous, information that excited the idealistic disciples of Henry David Thoreau and Walt Whitman and started them thinking about the possibility of preserving those wonders. (The reports also confirmed earlier declarations by trappers and prospectors that the land was too high, too mountainous, and too harsh to be suitable for homesteading and that it contained no extraordinary wealth of natural resources.) Another group—the officials of the Great Northern Railroad and influential citizens of the territories of Montana and Wyoming—saw the potential of this economically

Bighorn ewes graze on the tundra.

A bull moose munches wildflowers.

The Lewis monkey-flower flourishes in a seepage area.

worthless area as a means for advancing their own aims. The Great Northern needed business for its new rail lines, and the territorial politicians needed a larger population to represent. They saw in the establishment of a national park an inducement to greater settlement of the area, thereby benefiting all their interests.

So it was that the idealists—who believed in preserving a portion of the country in its natural state—and the opportunists—who wanted more commercial activity in the Rockies—found themselves working toward the same end. And, despite their different motivations, that end was realized when, in 1872, an act of Congress established Yellowstone National Park.

Established, but not funded. There was no money for either the protection or development of this "pleasuring ground for the people," as the act called it. For fourteen years the park was both inaccessible to most people and too accessible for exploitation by market game hunters and by trophy collectors. That condition led to the next period and its dominant groups.

1886 to 1917: The Cavalry and the Engineers

In 1886, making use of a legislative provision contained in an 1883 bill, the Secretary of the Interior called upon the Secretary of War for assistance in protecting the national park entrusted to his care and that had been, in the intervening years, so much abused. So for the next thirty-two years Yellowstone was administered jointly by the Interior Department and the War Department and was protected by cavalry units of the United States Army. During that same period many roads and buildings—some of which are still being used today—were planned and constructed by army engineers.

Still there was little money specifically appropriated for the park, but the combination of that little plus army "housekeeping" funds and investments by concessioners gradually increased Yellowstone's accessibility and expanded its facilities. By the end of the Army's period of administration the park closely resembled the national park it is today, and it was receiving an average of 10,000 visitors a year.

1918 to the Present: The Park Service and the People

In 1916 the National Park Service was created within the Interior Department for the special purpose of administering the fifteen national parks that then existed. In 1918 a Park Service ranger force, under Chester A. Lindsley, acting superintendent, then Horace M. Albright as superinten-

dent, took over the administration of Yellowstone. Budgets were still extremely limited and they had to continue to look to concessioners for funds. But the creation of a professional corps with a specific responsibility for the parks was, fifty-four years after the Yellowstone Park Act of 1872, a significant step toward the realization of the basic purpose of that legislation.

Today, park visitation is about 2.5 million a year, visitors who are very much aware of what such a park means to them. As wild America dwindles toward the vanishing point the protected islands of the natural world become ever more precious. The National Park Service, acting in accordance with its official responsibility, and the American people, recognizing their responsibility to mankind, together are continuing to ensure the preservation of Yellowstone National Park, the first of such protected islands.

SUGGESTED READING

CLARY, DAVID A. *The Place Where Hell Bubbled Up.* Washington, D.C.: U.S. Government Printing Office, 1972.

HAINES, AUBREY L. *The Yellowstone Story.* Boulder: Colorado Associated Universities Press, 1977.

———. *Yellowstone National Park, Its Exploration and Establishment.* Washington, D.C.: U.S. Government Printing Office, 1974.

Indian paintbrush flashes brilliantly against a dramatic backdrop—Lewis Falls.

Yellowstone Today

For over a hundred years Yellowstone National Park has been a sociological laboratory in which the people of America have been investigating—unconsciously for most—the meaning of the national-park concept, a concept that, superficially at least, is simple to define at any given time. But parks are a product of the American culture and that culture is not a static one. So parks today are

Norris Geyser Basin

not what they were yesterday—and tomorrow there will be other differences.

The somewhat conflicting purposes contained in the act establishing Yellowstone National Park —to "protect and preserve" the area and to keep it a place "for the benefit and enjoyment of the people"—have always required a certain amount of compromise.

An area cannot be preserved in its natural state if it is intruded upon by roads, hotels, service stations, campgrounds, and sewage plants. Nor can most people enjoy a park as large as Yellowstone if they are allowed to enter it only on foot and stay only until nightfall. Obviously some compromise is necessary—some alteration of the natural world must take place in order to accommodate the people by whom and for whom the park was

established. The question, then, is—and always has been—*how much* modification of the natural features is justifiable in the interest of human accessibility and convenience. The answer is complicated by the additional requirement of the National Park Service Act of 1916 to "leave it unimpaired for the enjoyment of future generations."

Over a hundred years ago Mammoth Hot Springs was the only one of the park's principal features that could easily be reached. Old Faithful and Yellowstone Canyon were each two additional days' travel by horse; Yellowstone Lake was yet another day beyond either of them. Park visitation was limited, but it could be seen that a system of roads and overnight accommodations would be needed—even at the expense of some modification of the natural state. The Grand Loop road and its related facilities were planned almost immediately after the park's establishment and were constructed as soon as funds were available. But American society has changed in those hundred years. Roads that were designed for horses and stagecoaches have been widened and regraded for use by automobiles. Facilities that were designed to accommodate only 10,000 visitors a year have been expanded to serve many times that number. Now, about 2.5 million people a year in a million motor vehicles use those facilities and roads—and the people and the park are again feeling the pressure.

For many years it has been generally felt that fishing is an appropriate recreational activity in a national park. To make the already good fishing here even better, several exotic species were introduced into the park's waterways. Their effects on

Park personnel and visitors alike will long remember Yellowstone's summer fires of 1988. Although ground fires usually move slowly through the undergrowth, when winds and intense heat combine as they did here the fire can suddenly jump into the treetops and race from tree to tree consuming miles of dry forest with frightening speed. Only the concentrated, heroic efforts of the firefighters (at one point nearly 10,000 were on duty) prevented loss of life and destruction of historic landmarks.

the ecosystem were not good, however, and today the Yellowstone fisheries are more carefully managed. It may even be true, as sometimes suggested, that in a national park—where the hunting of game animals, the picking of flowers, and the collecting of rocks are considered incompatible with preservation—the catching of fish may also be inappropriate.

Yellowstone's herds of game animals were protected from hunting as early as 1883, but annual "cropping" was practiced until the late 1960s, and predatory animals were "controlled" by official killing as late as the 1930s. Today it is believed that human control of predators is not only unnatural, it is also unnecessary. And wildlife biologists are investigating the possibility that the herds of ungulates, too, may need no management by people.

In addition, ecologists have long understood that fire, despite its role as "mankind's ancient enemy," is a natural part of the natural world and has been around as long as there has been fuel to burn, lightning to ignite it, and rain and snow to put it out. It is a force for *normal* change, and the *absence* of fire produces *abnormal* changes in the vegetative cover (remember that variety of lodgepole pine that *needs* fire to release its seeds?), and thereby affects all life in the community.

Nonetheless, the Park Service mission of protection requires that it suppress and control all human-caused fires and any other fires that are dangerously severe or threaten humans and their facilities. So each year in Yellowstone dozens of lightning strikes and some cases of human carelessness result in only a few hundred burned acres. Until the summer of 1988.

The weather that summer was unusually hot and rainless, and dry storms produced high winds and much lightning. The lodgepole forests were several hundred years old and contained many standing dead trees and much downed timber. For several preceding winters the snowfall had been below average, causing the moisture content of both the ground and the trees themselves to be excessively low.

So that summer, as inevitably as if it had used an earthquake or a volcanic eruption, the natural world used fire to bring about changes in the Yellowstone landscape. Hot, gale-force winds drove flames relentlessly through the dry forest. $120 million and the heroic efforts of a total of nearly 25,000 firefighters could do little but protect developed areas. In the park 1,000,000 acres burned, together with 250,000 acres of surrounding national forest land. As a result, although about half of Yellowstone still looks nearly as it did when the park was

YELLOWSTONE NATIONAL PARK

N

North Entrance
1620 m
5314 ft

Gardiner

MONTANA
WYOMING

Electric Peak

Cooke City

Road within the park between the North
Entrance and Cooke City is open all year.

MONTANA
WYOMING

Mammoth Hot Springs
Park Headquarters

Little Quadrant Mountain

Baronnette Peak

Northeast Entrance
2245 m 7365ft

Abiathar Peak

Slough Creek

GALLATIN RANGE

Golden Gate
Bunsen Peak

Blacktail Plateau

BLACKTAIL DEER PLATEAU

Blacktail Plateau Drive

Tower-Roosevelt

Pebble Creek

Druid Peak

The Thunderer

Quadrant Mountain

Bunsen Peak Road

Petrified Tree

Roosevelt Lodge

Mount Norris

Cache Mountain

Indian Creek

Antler Peak

Sheepeater Cliff

Prospect Peak

Tower Fall

SHOSHONE NATIONAL FOREST

GARDNERS HOLE

Dome Mountain

Obsidian Cliff

Mount Holmes

Mount Washburn

SPECIMEN RIDGE

LAMAR VALLEY

MIRROR PLATEAU

Observation Peak

Dunraven Pass

Roaring Mountain

Twin Lakes

Parker Peak

Saddle Mountain

Norris Geyser Basin

Museum

Canyon Village

GRAND CANYON OF THE YELLOWSTONE

Approximate Caldera Boundary

Inspiration Point
Artist Point

Norris

Pollux Peak

Steamboat Geyser

Lower Falls
Upper Falls

Wraith Falls

Castor Peak

Beryl Spring

HAYDEN VALLEY

White Lake

Pelican Cone

MONTANA
WYOMING

MADISON VALLEY

Road closed
from about
Nov. 1 to April 30

Madison

Gibbon Falls

Sulphur Caldron

Mud Volcano

Pyramid Peak

West Entrance
2032 m 6667ft

Mount Haynes

National Park Mountain

CENTRAL PLATEAU

PELICAN VALLEY

**Fishing Bridge,
Lake Village,
and Bridge Bay**

Fishing Bridge

Indian Pond

Firehole Canyon Drive

Fountain Flat Drive

ABSAROKA RANGE

Fountain Paint Pot

Three Senses Trail

Firehole Lake Drive

Great Fountain Geyser

Beach Lake

Bridge Bay

Lake Village

Steamboat Point

STEVENSON ISLAND

Mary Lake

Turbid Lake

Lower Geyser Basin

Goose Lake

Natural Bridge

Bicycle Trail

Lake Butte

Imperial Geyser

Midway Geyser Basin

Fairy Falls

YELLOWSTONE LAKE

Lake Elevation 2357 m 7733ft
Maximum Depth 98 m 320ft

Avalanche Peak

Cody Peak

East Entrance
2119 m 6951ft

Mystic Falls

Upper Geyser Basin

Mallard Lake

De Lacy Lake

Sylvan Pass

Road closed
from about
Nov. 1 to April 30

Biscuit Basin

Pumice Point

DOT ISLAND

Grizzly Peak

Top Notch Peak

Reservation Peak

Black Sand Basin

Old Faithful

Kepler Cascades

2258m
8391ft

**West Thumb
and Grant Village**

West Thumb

FRANK ISLAND

Mount Doane

Mount Langford

Lone Star Geyser

Scaup

Grant Village

Delusion Lake

Mount Stevenson

Mount Schurz

Summit Lake

SHOSHONE LAKE

Middle Lake

Eagle Pass

Coffer Peak

Eagle Peak
3462 m 11358ft
(Highest point in park)

Table Mountain

Lewis Lake

CONTINENTAL DIVIDE

SOUTH ARM

THE PROMONTORY

SOUTHEAST ARM

Turret Mountain

PITCHSTONE PLATEAU

RED MOUNTAINS

Mount Sheridan

Overlook Mountain

Heart Lake

Chipmunk Creek

Grouse Creek

Trail Lake

TWO OCEAN PLATEAU

THE TRIDENT

Dunanda Falls

CASCADE CORNER

Ouzel Falls

Colonnade Falls

Ranger Lake

Union Falls

89

191

Road closed
from about
Nov. 1 to April 30

Beula Lake

Hering Lake

Moose Falls

Buffalo Lake

MADISON PLATEAU

Approximate Caldera Boundary

Bechler

Cave Falls

BECHLER

South Entrance
2099 m 6886ft

Flagg Ranch

Snake River

JOHN D. ROCKEFELLER, JR.
MEMORIAL PARKWAY

287

NATIONAL FOREST

IDAHO
MONTANA

WYOMING

VICINITY MAP

Bozeman

191

90

89

MONTANA
WYOMING

YELLOWSTONE NATIONAL PARK

Cody

14

GRAND TETON NAT'L PARK

IDAHO

191

Jackson

15

N

YELLOWSTONE
NATIONAL PARK

established in 1872, the other half again looks as it probably did in the decades following the 1750s when the last great conflagration is believed to have swept the area.

Changes in the natural world, in human knowledge, and in human societies are inevitable. But, throughout all of the changes that are to come, Yellowstone National Park will continue to occupy the sociological niche it has always filled—that of a wild area that is being protected for the enjoyment of people. And it is a laboratory in which to test the policies and develop the techniques by which protection and enjoyment can be made compatible, so that Yellowstone—and all the national parks that have come since Yellowstone—will continue to operate for the benefit of mankind.

SUGGESTED READING

DeGolia, Jack. *Fire: The Story Behind A Force of Nature.* Las Vegas, Nevada: KC Publications, Inc., 1989.

Everhart, William C. *The National Park Service.* New York: Praeger Publications, 1972.

Tilden, Freeman. *Interpreting Our Heritage.* Chapel Hill: University of North Carolina Press, 1957.

Tilden, Freeman. *The National Parks.* New York: Alfred A. Knopf Publishers, 1968.

Books in the Story Behind the Scenery series: Acadia, Alcatraz Island, Arches, Blue Ridge Parkway, Bryce Canyon, Canyon de Chelly, Canyonlands, Cape Cod, Capitol Reef, Channel Islands, Civil War Parks, Colonial, Crater Lake, Death Valley, Denali, Dinosaur, Everglades, Fort Clatsop, Gettysburg, Glacier, Glen Canyon-Lake Powell, Grand Canyon, Grand Canyon-North Rim, Grand Teton, Great Smoky Mountains, Haleakala, Hawaii Volcanoes, Independence, Lake Mead-Hoover Dam, Lassen Volcanic, Lincoln Parks, Mount Rainier, Mount Rushmore, Mount St. Helens, National Park Service, National Seashores, North Cascades, Olympic, Petrified Forest, Redwood, Rocky Mountain, Scotty's Castle, Sequoia-Kings Canyon, Shenandoah, Statue of Liberty, Theodore Roosevelt, Virgin Islands, Yellowstone, Yosemite, Zion.
NEW: In Pictures — The Continuing Story: Bryce Canyon, Death Valley, Everglades, Grand Canyon, Sequoia-Kings Canyon, Yellowstone, Zion.

Published by KC Publications · Box 14883 · Las Vegas, NV 89114

Printed by Dong-A Printing and Publishing, Seoul, Korea
Color Seperations By Kwangyangsa Co., Ltd.